prince of hearts

raegan fordemwalt

Andrews McMeel
PUBLISHING®

for

mom and dad

Andrews McMeel Publishing
a division of Andrews McMeel Universal
1130 Walnut Street, Kansas City, Missouri 64106

www.andrewsmcmeel.com

25 26 27 28 29 TEN 10 9 8 7 6 5 4 3 2 1

ISBN: 978-1-5248-9512-9

Library of Congress Control Number: 2024941157

Editor: Danys Mares
Art Director/Designer: Tiffany Meairs
Production Editor: Kayla Overbey
Production Manager: Beth Steiner

ATTENTION: SCHOOLS AND BUSINESSES
Andrews McMeel books are available at quantity discounts with bulk purchase for educational, business, or sales promotional use. For information, please email the Andrews McMeel Publishing Special Sales Department: sales@amuniversal.com.

contents

don't be afraid
to love with everything.

1: princess of heartbreak

a fairy tale

it's always been my dream to
be somebody's princess.
fairy-tale kisses and pretty white dresses.
i feel like a kid again thinking of it,
but i wish it didn't make me sick,

because i've stopped believing in
true love and castles,
glass slippers and fairy tales—i get it now.
fairy tales are not real,
stories are just stories,

and apples always sour.

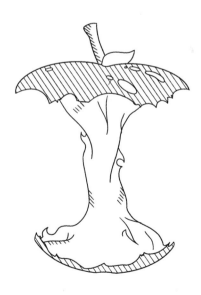

somebody's crush

i could never be somebody's crush.
i could never be the *romantic interest*
in some boy's story.

i'm not pretty enough to
have that kind of love.
that kind of love where he smiles at you
and says, *you're so beautiful.*

i'm not pretty enough
to be wanted from afar.
pined after, pursued.
sure, someone will love me eventually,
but they'll have to know me,
and maybe that's not so bad, but

♥

is it too much to want to be wanted like
boys want the pretty girls?
to be wanted like i see on tv?

i just want someone to have a crush on me.
someone's crush.
someone's girl.

keep writing

it's the only part of me that
didn't leave when they did.
they took my love, and
they ate it like a compliment,
but they can't take my poetry.
they didn't take all of me.

it's mine. it's still mine.
i keep my wounds fresh.

keep writing.
keep writing.

i'm princess of nothing but that.

you haven't left your room in days

you haven't left your room in days.
you don't mind. it's strange:
the thought that all you need
is your phone
and your poems
and the internet
to feel as if you're okay.

but you haven't left your room in days.
there's something wrong with that, baby.

you were supposed to have been better by now.

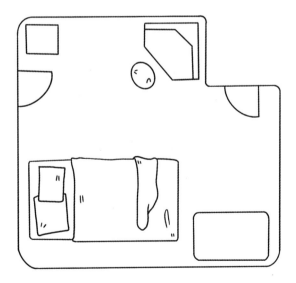

lover girl, again

the lover girl
is the princess of heartbreak.
she wants a savior, but
she's afraid of being saved.

her heart is too ugly,
too fragile,
to be held in anyone's hands
but her own.

used

i see a used girl
in bad condition.

i will never again be anything but
the thing someone
didn't want.

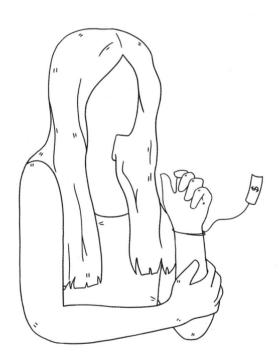

heart-break

i guess i hadn't realized
being *heartbroken*
really meant
i broke my heart.

it doesn't work the way it's supposed to.
it's not functional, not operational—
i can't do it like i used to.
i can't love, not like before.

pity her:
the lover girl not able to
love anyone
anymore.

one paragraph

i feel stupid for feeling
so deeply scarred by
one paragraph i was sent
over a year ago.
it's just words.

but these are too,
and i still can't stop writing.

i must have it memorized by now.

infinite

i used to believe that love was infinite.
like a well between my breasts that would never dry
and leave me full.
but here i am,
and i've forgotten how a bath feels,
and i've forgotten how it feels to
be held in someone's arms.

and maybe it's true.
maybe love is infinite, but
it's not a well between my breasts
wetting the hands i hold yours in—
it's my blood. my neck, my hips,
sticky, drying, bleeding out of me,
leaving me ever weak and
making me deathly thirsty.

i will never bleed out
from my love,
but the wounds will never heal.

bleeding hearts are fatal for girls like me,
but i won't let mine scab over yet.

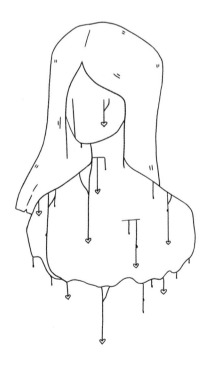

the girl in love

who was that girl
in love last summer?

i've forgotten who i am,
because the most i've ever felt like myself
was when i was holding the hand of a man.

who am i
if not in love?

un-broken

i have spent so long
un-breaking my heart
that i don't know what to do with
the part of it i fixed all on my own.
i've got nobody to show it off to,
but even then,

i'm still embarrassed at the state of it.

someone loves you

it's the worst feeling
to think someone loves you,
to think someone is your best friend,
your person,
and realize that
they don't even like you.
that maybe they never did,
and they just never told you until now.

and you wonder
how many other people
still just have not told you yet?

unwanted

i never cancel plans. i never even think of it.
i never say no,
i never want to.
i try to show them that i love them.
i try too hard and they always leave,
but it's okay.
it's okay, i think,
because at least they
don't feel the same way i did.

at least they don't feel unwanted.

love will come to me

i scream this like i mean it.
i repeat it in the mirror.
a poem i wrote
four years ago,
like it still means anything,
like it still matters.

love will come to me.
love will come to me.

i whisper,
please.

knight of my heart

i sit alone again
writing poems.
all i do is write and
wait. waiting for the
knight of my heart
to come and save me.

it has to be me

because everyone has left.
everyone has gone and
i see the pattern's end.
i know things like that don't happen by accident.
i'm the only constant,
the only other element.
i know people don't just leave.
it doesn't add up.
it's me. it has to be.

i am nobody's person

i am nobody's person. i am not the first one
anyone would think to text
when something happens.
i am not the one
you'd take if you had two tickets
to some random event.
i'm not the first choice.
i used to be,
but now i'm just used.
overlooked.

i'm nobody's person anymore.

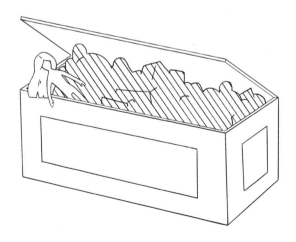

used to be me

i see them walk into class together every day.
he pulls her seat out for her, and
she makes fun of him and takes it anyway.
i see them link hands as they walk out
and remember the weight of his hand in my own.

and i don't want his to fill it, i just want
to stop feeling like it's wrong that it's empty.
i need to stop looking at her
and thinking

that used to be me.

something to write down

i wear makeup only because
that's what i used to do
when i was with you.
i'm not a person if i'm not in love or heartbroken.
i'm nothing if i'm not something i can write down.

i am just an imitation of who i was
back when i was in love.

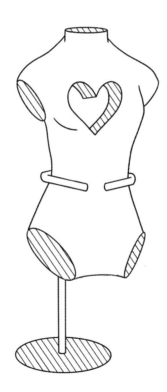

when i came home

always alone.
just me and my phone.
i write poetry like
it's all i have left in me.
i write until my eyes ache and my
fingers bleed.

you said you'd be here when i came home.

pretty parts

there are no more
pretty parts in a lover girl like me.

i spent all my pretty parts
on people who kept them
like they were nothing but a gift.
i'm empty.

and i say it's their fault, but
they didn't even want them to begin with.

ha! i was a pretty girl,
but the lover girl is all that's left.

♥

leaving me

i'm not conventionally pretty.
i'm not easy to brag about.
i'm a little overbearing,
and i talk too loudly in quiet rooms.
i'm gross. i'm inappropriate. i'm petty.
my heart is misshaped. wet. fumbling.
covered in dried blood and bile,
it's hard to hold on to.
hard to keep wanting to.

i don't blame them, not really.
a misshaped heart doesn't fit between
most people's hands.
it wouldn't even in my own.

♥

too much love

there is such a thing as "too much" love,
because you feel it when you
realize you would have done for a friend
what they never would have done for you.
when you realize
it doesn't work like that,
that love isn't equal. it never really is,
and you're always the one
giving too much.

me too

i wouldn't have wanted to be my friend, either,
looking back on it.

i can't play the victim
like i always try to,
because you and i are the same.

i never would have done that to you.
but, god,
i would have done it to me too.

nobody's time

i take up nobody's time,
not even my mother's, anymore.
i make sure not to bother her.
i know she's busy with my brother.

i take up nobody's time but my own.
i do well in school.
i'm quiet at home.
i've been good. i've been so good.

i take up nobody's time but my own.

love once

i am so terrified that
i will never love again like
the way i did. the way i used to.
i used it up:
my first love ticket.

for the rest of my life,
it will only ever be his.

and i'm not afraid i'll never fall in love again.
i know it's possible,
i'm just afraid that every new love will be only
a pale imitation of what i had.
each kiss will be him,
each smile,
each *i love you*
will be like i'm looking into his eyes.

i will see him and remember
he loved me just the same and
left me just the same.

how will i be able to love after
learning how it feels to lose it?

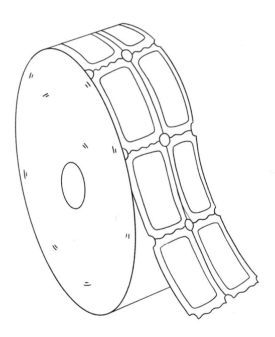

how to be in love

i've been in love a few too many times
i'm a lover girl, i don't think i can help it.
i give my heart too freely to friends and strangers.
people who don't know me
and don't want to.

and even after all this time
i've not learned
how to be in love.
i've not learned how to love without being selfish.
how to love without making it all about me.

something's missing

something's missing.
i feel it when i'm driving.
i see it in my lock screen.
i hold it on swing sets and the space left between.
because i feel it worse when
i realize i would be holding his hand
even though i don't know who he is.

something's missing.
he's missing.

what you wrote for me

do you remember when
sticky notes covered the surface of
all my walls?
i wrote most of them late at night,
when ideas for poems would
come into my mind
that i knew i would forget
by the morning.

i asked you to write me one.
do you remember that?
it's still somewhere in the journal i put them all in.
i never let anyone else do that.

i'm too afraid to go through them now in case i find it.
i don't want to know what you wrote
back when you still loved me.

only the worst things

i am made of
only the worst things,
i've been told by
the people i loved the most.

time

you take up all my time,
and i vowed

i would never again be a burden.
not to anyone.
not anymore.
i would never again be a chore.

and i did,
or at least i tried to.
i stopped inviting friends out.
they would say yes only
because they felt like they had to.
and you did, didn't you?
you couldn't tell me no
you said it like this
you take up all my time.

♥

so i stopped texting people,
taking up their time.
i didn't take up any time.
only mine. i took up only mine.

i take up no time.

lover girl loves too hard

it's always been her problem:
loving too much.
loving like a grudge.
like a promise. like a *compliment*.
she loves like she thinks it'll be enough.

shards of glass

i can feel it sometimes
when i breathe.

my heart is no longer broken,
but the pieces of what it used to be
rattle inside me.

i think you could hear it
if you were ever to get close enough.

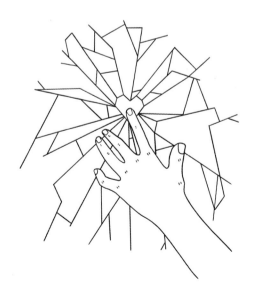

love isn't real

because
someone can know you
so completely,
read your poetry every thursday,
help you write plays,
spend hours in your car or in your house,
and still, after it all,
dislike you.

they knew you the best of anyone,
they watched in awe,
because they stared into your mind,
into your heart,
and hated what they saw.

♥

princess of heartbreak

princess of heartbreak.
isn't it funny?
i guess it's better than being a princess of nothing.
but now she's alone in her tower,
and the blood that she spilt over her window's ledge is
killing the grass at the base of it.
nobody wants to come close.

"i used to be happy"

i used to be happy,
i say aloud,
and i didn't know the words
used to be
would make me realize it was true.

i used to be happy,
and my friends stared at me, silently,
and i pretended not to see their pitying eyes.
i was fine.
i was just fine.

i smiled.

i chose this

i didn't have to let anyone in.
i didn't have to be a poet.
i didn't have to fall in love
or make a habit of telling everyone about it.

i should stop pretending i'm the victim of the
ones who took my heart and squeezed.

i am just as much to blame.
i have to be.

stars in the sky

he loved me once,
and i loved him more than
the stars in the sky.

but i saw one falling today.
i didn't bother making a wish, but
it burned down the world when it landed anyway.

there are no more stars in the sky.

no more love

if i never fall in love again,
i won't have to fall *out* of it.

i like that thought.
no more love.

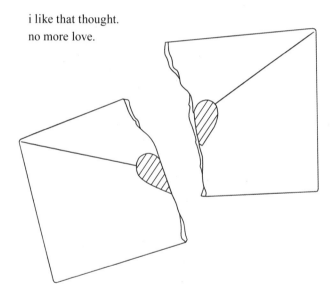

2: her and her dandelion crown

someone here

there's twenty thousand people at this school,
fifty thousand in this city.
there has to be someone here, at least one
who thinks that i'm pretty.
a prince just for me.

but what if there really is nobody,
and i've just been
waiting.

waiting for my prince of hearts to save me.
waiting for nobody to come and save me.

♥

supposed to be

i'm such a mess, i'd feel pity
for any new person i love and who loves me,
because wouldn't that just be such a party?
scrambling beside me,
holding me carefully,
making sure not to break open the cracks,
barely healed.

loving is supposed to come naturally,
but only if they love
anyone but me.

talking to myself

i don't miss him.
i just miss how he knew
everything about me,
because if i've got nobody that knows me,
what am i at all but my poetry?

he listened to everything about me,
he became every vowel, every sentence, every noun,

and now that he's gone, i have a thousand poems
but nothing to write down.

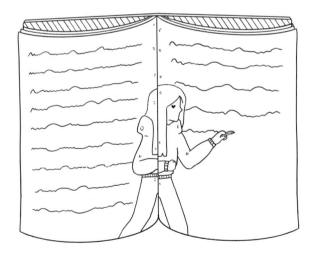

♥

2:00 a.m. poem, part two

i'm alone writing this,
the room is dark, and i like pretending i'm
invisible to the people passing by.

someone will love me soon.
i write it and it doesn't feel true.
but that's what this poem is about, isn't it?
the idea of anyone,
the idea that i won't always be alone.

♥

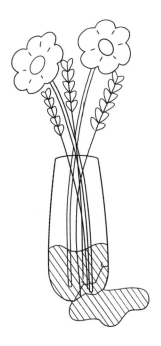

flowers meant to die anyway

i feel like i'm ready. i look like i am.
i am. i am.
but what if i find him and
i've been broken all along?
what if i'm temporary in the same way that

valentine's flowers always die.

♥

sick of loving me

i know what you're wanting to read is
that the key to love
is to love yourself.
that's all it takes to be happy, right?
loving yourself like you'd love anyone else.

but i can't write that,
not without it sounding like a lie.
i've spent so long "healing,"
getting better, being single.
i'm so sick of loving myself.
i'm so sick of needing help.

i want a surprise party.
i want someone to buy me jewelry.
i want my hand to be held when someone
knows something is wrong.
i want a road trip out of nowhere.
i want to be sent stupid videos of dogs.

i want to be thought about,
i want to be known,
i want not to have to love myself
all on my own.

so i can't just write that
all you need is to love yourself.
it's so much work.
i'm so much work.
i'm getting tired.

and, god, how long will i be able to
hold my own heart
before my arms give out?

how heartbreak feels

i've forgotten how heartbreak feels,
and i guess that should be a good thing,
but i miss the dying. i miss the hurt,
because now i just feel nothing.

i used to pine after him like a ghost
never leaving her own grave.
i used to love like a curse, and
i used to be afraid.
but now i just feel empty. bitter.

i've stopped loving him.
and, somehow, heartbreak was better.

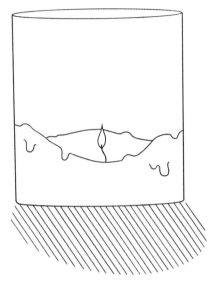

none of me

there's none of me left.
used girl. dying flame.

♥

worst parts of me

i look for the worst parts of myself in everyone now.
i look for the heartbreak in their eyes.
i look for shadows by their side,
things they haven't yet left behind.

it's everyone and me, and i find terrible things
like each one is a prize.

♥

bees

shouldn't i be a flower attracting bees?
why have they come to everyone but me?

am i not yet broken enough
to want to save?

to like you

i just want to like you.
i don't even want to be loved back, not now.
i just want proof that it can happen again.

i want proof that when i think of love,
i won't always think of him.

behind

i feel like i'm behind.

there's this girl i know
who met her boyfriend in high school.
they went to the same college.
they have it all figured out.
she wears a promise ring.
spoiled her own surprise. she doesn't mind.

i feel like i'm behind.

♥

girlfriend girl

i'm a girlfriend girl,
and i don't want to hook up with boys or
have an *almost* with some kid in my class.
no, i want a boyfriend.
that's all i ask.

because i'm not a casual lover.
i'm a lover girl.
i want a boyfriend. not a more-than-friends.
not a one-night or an option.
i want him, but i want all of him
or nothing at all.

and if he wants something else,
if he just wants a casual love,
he can have that.
go find that,
just find it with someone who wants that too.
go have a casual love
with anyone but me.

wearing red

they tell me to just be myself,
be natural, be normal—
they tell me not to force it,
but i'm among the wolves now, wearing red.
i wonder if they can smell the blood
still staining my hands.

♥

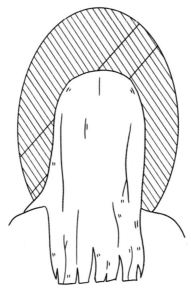

pretty

i can't tell if i'm pretty or not.
i can't tell if others like me.
i stare at my face in the mirror

and what a mess it is. look at the asymmetry.
each freckle dots the cheeks.
each pimple is a spot of red on pale skin.
the curve of uneven breasts, uneven hips.
big nose. red tongue. two eyes and two ears.

♥

it's moving now. it shows straight white teeth:
a body made to live and reproduce and eat.

a collection of carbon atoms.
they make geometry. spheres on cones and cylinders.
mass over volume. density.

distorted darkness. look at it.
yellow and red and green.

a color, a shape, a body, a girl.

how pretty.

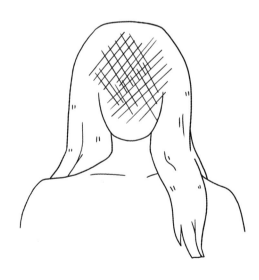

be me

maybe i'm just angry,
or jealous, seeing happy couples
pass by me,
but i'm bitter because i'm lonely,
and i'm mean like
i somehow deserve to be.
it could be me, why isn't it me?

♥

spoiling it

i'm putting together every perfect thing
impossible for any boy to be.
contradictory.

i'm spoiling myself.
spoiling the ending.
the one where i find out
he doesn't exist.

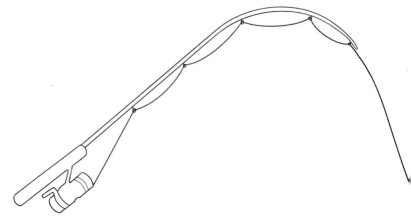

excited to be alone

a part of me was excited,
just a little bit,
because i never would have left you,
but then when you did,
i could do anything i wanted.
i could meet someone who isn't you and
like them more.

you left me, so it was my chance to be
even more happy, right?
prove to you i don't need you, that i never did.
i could thank you at the end because
you left me and i needed it.

♥

raegan fordemwalt

but the truth is that
even though i've pumped my own heart back
to where blood is flowing through my cheeks,

i'm still just as lonely as i was before you left me.

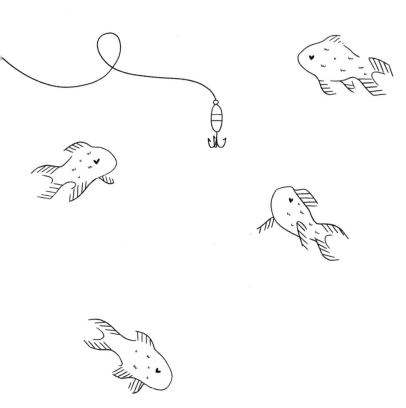

♥

what love is like

my heart beats so weakly,
i've had to reach between my own ribs to revive it,
i've broken my bones
and chewed them like a dog.
i've made myself wrong.
i've made myself fall in love.

everything since then has been empty.

ten crushes

i have ten crushes.
i count them out and write them down like
their names are mine.

i have ten crushes.
i have none.
i'm just addicted to the taste of
almost falling in love.

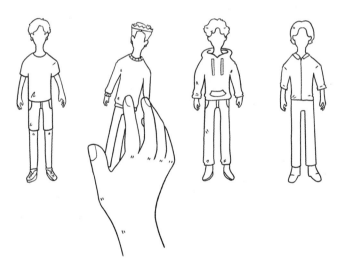

animals

even if a boy just looks my way,
even if i'm someone he'd never see,
i see him and i categorize him like an animal.
it makes me sick, but what am I
if not an animal too?

even the birds' songs have started to sound like
they were written just for me.

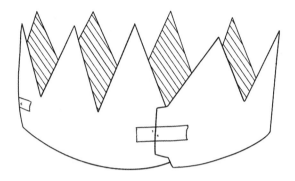

set me up

my friends keep saying they want to
set me up with someone,
but it feels like a children's game. childish.
like i'm a doll inside their homemade dollhouse,
but the prince is made of paper and
glitter glue.

♥

kissed her anyway

i didn't mean to stare. i couldn't help it.
he grabbed her waist, and she shrieked.
she jumped from his hands with a smile.
he kissed her anyway. he whispered something, and
she blushed and pushed him away.
i bet he thinks she's prettiest like that.
i bet he makes her blush like that every day.

i stare and want him to never kiss her again.

♥

prescription

i went on a date today.
i didn't like him before,
and he didn't like me.
my therapist said to say yes.
but it felt chemical. a prescription
to make myself seen.

i'm choking down the pills, but
dates just make me feel more lonely.
and if it's just me who's sickly,
what's the need?

♥

dry lips

something about it is wrong.
my blood is solid. my clothes are liquid.
i'm soaking wet everywhere else, but
i like the crack of my dry lips.

my heart beats down to my fingertips,
but i hold his hand in mine
and feel nothing.

♥

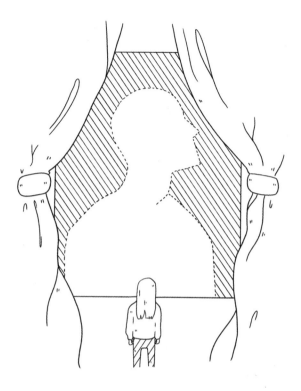

can't like him

look at him.
isn't he perfect?
beating heart and breathy laugh.
he's everything i dreamed he'd be, so
why aren't there stars in his eyes?

aren't i a lover girl? isn't that what i'm meant to do?

isn't he what i wanted?

roller coasters

i hate roller coasters
not because i'm afraid of heights.
no, i'm afraid of the lines.

i've always wanted to be
at the front of the ride,
and i could have made it,
if only i stood
just one step ahead or one behind.

all my life
what have i missed out on
at the back of the ride?

can't kiss him

he tried to kiss me, and i blew air onto his lips.
his eyes opened in rejection, and
i saw myself become nobody within them.

i can't kiss him because
it has to be better than what i used to have
or else i loved for nothing.

love stories

things like that
happen only in stories. they're why stories exist.

i imagine myself as the heroine. the princess.
i'm waiting for my love story. i'm waiting
for the happily ever after,
but i'm just a writer,
and my pen cannot love me back.

♥

everything matters now

everything matters now.
i need to fix my instagram,
fix my hair.
i need to wear makeup to class,
i need to post online and look pretty like i care.

everything matters now because it takes just
one person to notice me for
everything to be okay again.

dandelion crown

i make myself a crown
with the dandelions in my backyard.

i pluck them like i'm saving them.
i place them in my filthy hair and preen.
my kingdom. my empire
i make just for me.
i scare everyone away as i
fill my head with weeds.

what a tragedy it would be
if they fell for the girl with the dandelion crown.
the one wearing dirt like she's royalty.

i try to be beautiful.
i try to be pretty.
but the bugs cover me
as caked foundation and mascara
leave tracks down my cheeks.

♥

how attractive I must be,
the girl in the dandelion crown,
but i'm drawing only bugs and fleas.

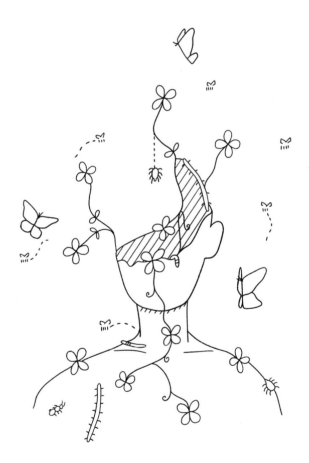

vanilla perfume

i bleed a sickly sweet vanilla perfume.
it's covering the floor now. leaking into it.
i like it, but my eyes are watering.
i breathe it in. i'll start to hate it soon.

i wonder,
if i held my breath,
how long i could stand it.

only chance

my hands shake writing it down:
i'll never fall in love again.
i convince myself it's true.
what if he just really was
the one for me?

what if i already ruined my only chance?

boys only love me when we're alone

boys only love me when we're alone.
when his hand's under my shirt and
his eyes are focused on my lips.
he only holds my hand when
he wants more attention.
he only says that he loves me when
he sees my naked waist.

because with others, he's distracted,
talking to friends,
too busy with work and school.
he can't make time for me.
i know that. i have to know that.
and so

as it ends,
i wait to be alone again
so he will love me just like
i love him.
just like i can't stop loving him.

boys only love me
when they touch me.
boys only love me when we're alone.

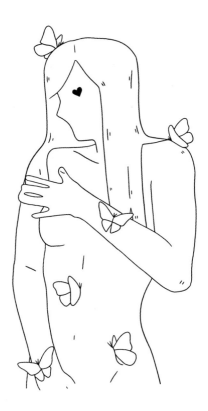

her prince

i watch them.
she doesn't know i dreamed of his eyes last night,
and i don't tell.

i hold my breath when they pass me by.
he doesn't look at me. never has, and
however much i wish i could see the eyes i dreamed of,
i never will.

they're locked on her.
he's her prince, not mine.

♥

too emotional

i write poetry like it doesn't scare boys away.

emotional girl. sensitive girl.
she'll write about you and put it online.
she'll fall for you and
cry if you don't buy her flowers.
she'll have sex with you only if you
date her too. ew.

nobody wants the girl filled with crazy words like *love*.

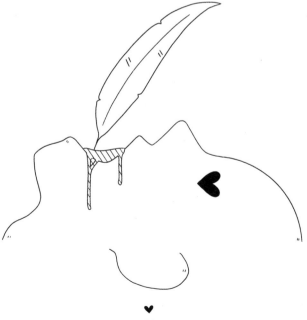

home

when my grandmother was at her worst with dementia,
she would look at my grandfather and repeat,
jim, i want to go home.
sitting in her own house
on her own bed.

she forgot her home. she forgot my father, me.
but she never forgot him.
even at the end, she said,
jim, i want to go home.

i wonder how much space a love must take
inside a heart
for it to be strong enough to outlast perception.
outlast disease. outlast home.

i like to think, even by the end,
even when he was all she remembered
and all she had,

it was enough.

♥

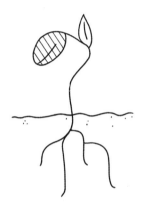

still works

i felt it again,
the jump inside my chest.
i had a dream of him, and i liked it.
i dreamt he was my everything, and
i woke up and couldn't have him.

my eyes still bleary from sleep,
and my ribs broken from the pound of it,
but my chest thrums, and i feel it—
i'm alive.
doesn't this mean something?
doesn't this mean my heart still works after all?

the heart that's easy to kill

i'm the girl you know you can charm.
i'm the heart that's easy to kill.
i'm the one who puts it all out there
even though i'm just standing still.

and it's you. it's always you
holding me at will again.
backing me up against walls and
pinning me there with your stare.
you've got me running,
you've got me scared,
you've got my everything, but
i don't even care.

because here i am again,
lost in your pretty eyes.
i'm the heart that's easy to kill,
and you're the boy with the knife.

♥

rotting me

it's that same feeling
when i realize
i've forgotten to take out the trash and
i had just gotten so used to the rotting smell.
i couldn't tell.

you've ruined me, and i hate
that i don't even mind.

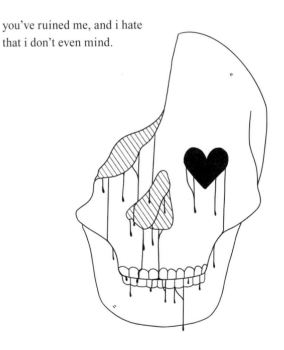

♥

just you

i want a boyfriend
but i don't want just a boyfriend,
i think. i want love.

i want him to tickle me from behind.
i want him to eat from my plate.
that kind of love where
he texts me when he sees a deer in the road.
i want him to watch stupid rom-coms with me
and pay attention because
i like talking about them afterward.
i want to be able to hang out with his friends
and without them.
i want him to buy me flowers.

i want the kind of love that heals me.
i want the love that creeps inside of me like
cold water down my fever-sick throat.

like the way it feels to be at the full height of
an elevator
or the pop of a balloon,
as confetti falls down to the ground.
i want him to love me like that.

my hands tremble as i write the truth.
i don't want a boyfriend.
i just want you.

♥

3: bittersweet

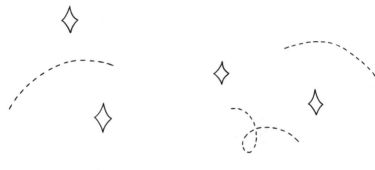

bittersweet

when he's gone, it's aching.

i'd forgotten what it felt like.
bittersweet, right?
the taste of love.

stars anyways

i'm here
writing this same poem again,
the one i always write when i've fallen in love.
i write about the stars and strings and
how my little heart beats.

isn't that terrible?
that i'll soon have to write that one i do
when it ends.
when you leave me too.

raegan fordemwalt

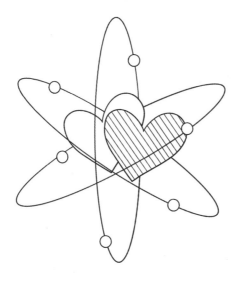

made from fire

there's this ball of light
bouncing around my chest cavity,
warming me,
moving me toward you. energy.

i touch you, and i feel electricity.

what i would give
to see my spark in you.

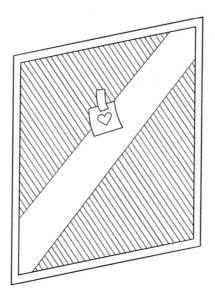

do you care?

do guys care?
do guys think about girls at two in the morning,
imagining his hand in hers?
do guys show photos of her to strangers,
asking if they think he has a chance?
do guys get nervous when she comes around?
do they stress over the outfit they're wearing and
update their friends on if she's replied yet?

do guys even tell their friends about her?
do they even talk about her—

♥

does he talk to his friends about me?
does he tell them exactly how many times i pass him
walking to class?
do his friends know i'm the *she* in all his stories?
do guys care?

do you care
like i do?

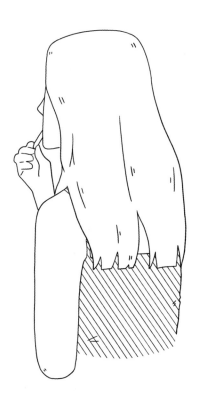

true love's kiss

i am poisoned, but
i imagine the antidote in your lips.
do it sweetly.
wake me up with true love's kiss.
i need you.
i was asleep until you found me.

♥

you and who i made you

i don't know you.
not really.
i just know enough to think about you
like i am now.
creating this love story like
it wouldn't upset you to read it.
i'm making you into something you're not.
i'm taking your image
and making you into the sky and the stars.

and how awful i am for it,
because
you will never know this poem
and i will never know you.

how unfair it is for me to love you and not know you.

♥

the poem hours after

you smile at me,
and i pretend it means more than just a greeting.

i pretend you'd smile like that every day if you
knew how it made my heart skip
and knew how i thought about it
even now,
hours after.

not going to hope

i am not going to hope for it.
even though i know, of course, i already love you.
in my daydreams, i spend
a million moments
trying to match your eyes
with the color of the sky,
but that's exactly why.

i am not going to hope for it.
i will not be in the ground again.
bury me alive.

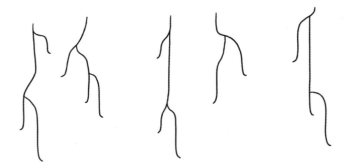

♥

honey sweet

you're the honey sweet for my starving lips.

i want you like i'm hungry for just a kiss.
i want you like i need it,
like i deserve it.

♥

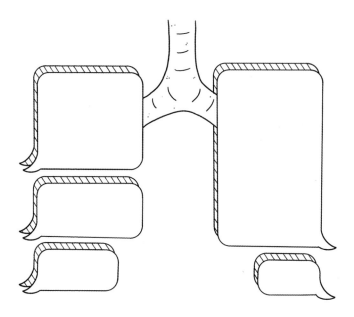

between messages

i've tried holding my breath
between each time you message me.
it helps me when it's painful.
when i run out of oxygen,
i forget.

♥

cornflower blue

i could spend forever staring into your eyes,
but i doubt you even know
the color of mine.

glass slipper

i would cut my toes,
break my bones,
stain the glass slipper with
black blood and bile
just to be someone you say you love.

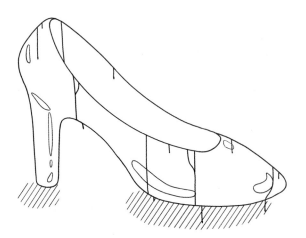

when my hands are empty

i have to hold on to something now,
for when my hand is empty,
i imagine you holding it.
i imagine you pressing your lips to the back of it,
i imagine how it would feel
to touch the hair at the nape of your neck.

and still,
no matter what i grasp between them,
every time i fill my palms,
it feels wrong.

grinning from the thought

i don't know if you're my prince.
i don't really care.
i'll take just a brush of your hand if it's all
you'll give me,
and i'll be happy for it.

beauty and the beast

i want you to change me.
i write it down, and i like the sound of it.
someone else saving me.
someone else doing all the work
just for me.

stitch me up. cure me. doctor me and
cut my hair.
make me nothing like i used to be.
i'll be anything as long as you'll have me.

leading me on

when will you get tired of leading me on?

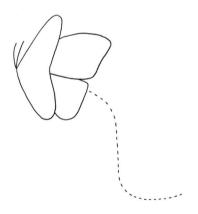

♥

sickly poem for you

i'm sick again, and i know
you could fix me if you were here.

i want you to not care.
i want you to still love me,
still want me,
even after all the work i am,
even after seeing me lost in my head—
i want you to still want me after that.

bleeding heart

i feel blood pool between my fingers
and pretend i'm bleeding for you.

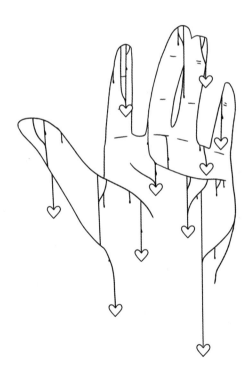

impossible us

i wish we weren't impossible.
i don't know,
there's something about you i like a lot,
something about us that i know would work,
i swear would work, but
of course we have to be impossible, and
of course it would be so funny.
of course it would.

i can't help playing with the idea in my mind.
it's a comfort, a little bit,
the thought that you will never be mine.
there are no consequences.
nothing's at stake if i lie.

♥

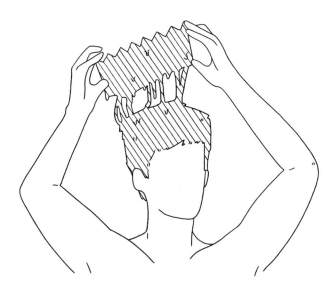

royalty

when i close my eyes and touch the hair on your head,
i feel a crown.

it suits you too well: royalty.

always like you more

i keep thinking of my parents.
they'd see it in my eyes,
my admiration,
my pull and drive.
they'd see me melt
and see how you don't move at all.

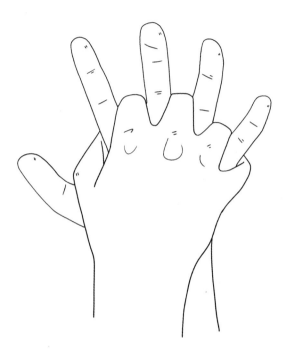

your hands and the end of the world

i wasn't supposed to like you.
i wasn't meant to. i'm not built for it,
for you,
but i write it down and i know it's true.
something beats down to my fingers
as i stare at your hand
wishing desperately that you'd hold mine.

♥

need you

i need to be with you.
i don't care—
i don't care if it's codependent or needy.
i really don't care as long as you're here,

because it doesn't matter if we're toxic.
because without you, i feel sick.
physically ill. unwell.
you must have noticed the rotting smell.

god, i need you.
and you know i do,
and you know you don't need me too.

raegan fordemwalt

smothered, dead

it'd been weeks, and
i thought you were gone.
i thought i was better.
i thought i'd moved on,

but just the sight of you
and it was as if i never tied you up at all.

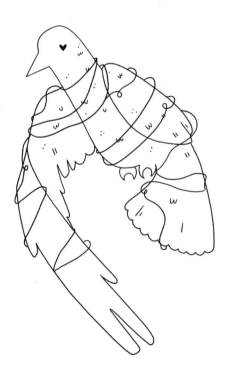

glass bones and you

my skeleton is made from glass bones.
they're hidden underneath me,
but if he ever were to hold my hand,
how would i explain the need
to be gentle?

to never ask

you have so much power over me.
if i had a choice,
i'd choose to never leave your arms.
so that is why you must never ask.
i do not want to be trapped with you

because i would say yes.
i would say yes.

the love thing

i've started to call it
"the love thing" in my head.
it's how i've fallen for you,
foolishly,
because i'm writing this poem for me, i tell myself,
and the lie tastes wrong on my tongue.
it's all for you. i'm all for you.

i'm thinking about the things i'll tell nobody else,
the things that make me swallow you whole.
i've kept myself so busy these past weeks,
for when i find myself alone,
my thoughts just wander back to you
and i get lost.

if i could squint and grab the sky to
tear it in two,
i'd find no sun,
i think i'd only find you.

the back of your car

i wanted to kiss you
so badly. i've never wanted anything as much.
i've never wanted it so much.

i wish i had,
but i'm glad i didn't,
because
you would have kissed me back.

❤

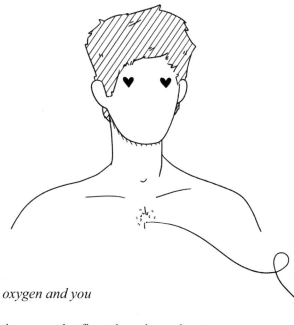

oxygen and you

the oxygen that flows through your heart
is the same that i breathe.
i can't live without your love inside me.

i want to swallow everything you swallow.
i want to curl up in your arms and between your legs.
i want to eat you. i want to love you,
and i want to stare into your eyes.

i want to touch you everywhere.
i want to kiss you. taste your teeth. i want to
be the thing always on your mind.

i want you to think of me always, and
when you do,
i am there. i never left.

i want to wear your clothes. i want to wear them
with you. i want to wear your skin and lungs.
i want to breathe your air.
i want everything.
i want all of it.
i want you.

if they knew you

you burn me
with every touch.
you consume my lungs and body.
my skin is red and blistering from your flame,
and everyone's saying they don't feel it,
but the wind sweeps me forward, and

i imagine you'd swallow the world
if they knew you
like i do.

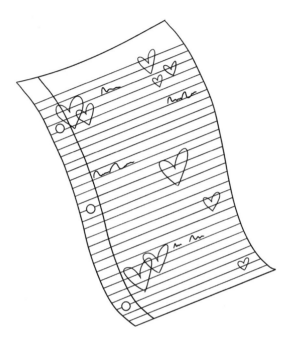

love again

lover girl is falling in love again,
and she wrote you this poem
because that's what love makes the lover girl do.
write. writing about you,
it's obsessive. creepy even,
but if you love the lover girl
like she thinks that you do,
you probably don't mind.

♥

love poem

i think i'm falling in love again.
it's a strange feeling.
no, it's not.
i'm a liar.
i recognized it right away.
i knew it once i tasted you that first time.
i knew it when i saw your smile in the moonlight.
i knew it. of course i knew it.
i'm a poet.
of course i'd know.

i'm falling in love again.
i know it.
i love you. i love you
and
i won't say it out loud.

as confetti falls down to the ground

it's never been this easy before,
and i know i shouldn't compare you
to the stars in the sky,
but i'm awful and i like you more.

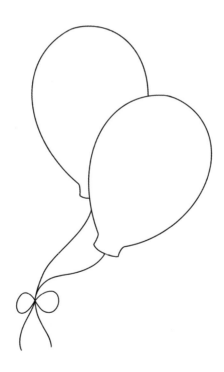

♥

love will come to you

love will come to you.
stop searching.

i get it.
you're wishing for anything that
will fill the gap inside your heart that
they made and left in you,

but forcing something, someone else in
will not fill it.
it will rip the edges,
make you bleed. you can't give yourself
stitches in a place your hands can't reach.

love will come to you.
and it will not happen like you expected,
but they will be everything you need.
you just have to stop looking.

"i love you"

did you catch how i almost said it?
i hope you didn't.
i hope you never know, and
i hope those words are never spoken from my mouth.
i can taste them after every time you smile,
every time you speak.
i can feel the words
i love you
bubbling inside of me every second i'm with you.

what if you don't say it back?

♥

4: prince of hearts

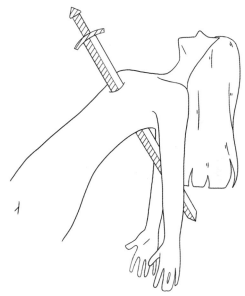

in the morning

in my dreams,
my knight in shining armor runs toward me.
you're dressed in metal white,

and your sword drags through my chest,
through my sternum, into my fragile heart,
ripping it out, still beating like
some grotesque piece of art.
i imagine you feel bad for hurting me,
you apologize, and i know you mean it.
i'm sorry— i'm sor—

i wake up to your good morning text.
how long before my dreams come true?

♥

learning you

i want to hold your arm without a second thought.
i want to have a place we always go for food.
i want to know your friends like they're mine.
i want to keep a toothbrush in your bathroom.

how jarring it is to move from having a relationship
where i knew him so deeply that, when he left,
he took nearly all of me,
to falling for you and having to wait for anything.

i'm sick of waiting for *loving* you
to stop being *learning* you.

ahead

you said it.
you said,
i love you too.

and i should be excited, but
i know the end of this story already.
i read the page ahead.

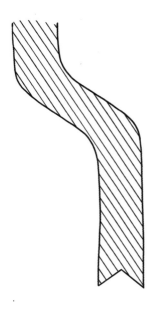

♥

headline

she's never had a healthy relationship.
you know this.
everyone does by now.

it's all she writes poetry about.

starting over

i know how it ends, but
i ask what your favorite color is.
you ask me mine.

it always starts like this,
and i've read this story a hundred times.
i know how the ending goes,
but for now, you just tell me

your favorite color is red.
so is mine.

roses die all the same.

find no sun

the stars ate me and spit me out.
they were so beautiful until i looked too long.

i'm making a habit of it:
stripping the beauty from everything i love.

♥

burden

a broken heart
is all i have to give to you.

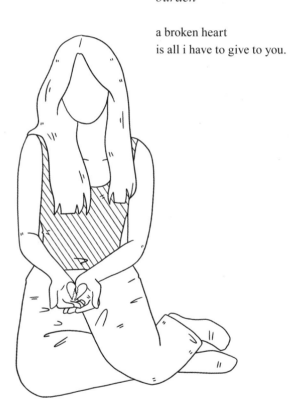

prince of hearts

true love's curse

everyone has left me
except you, yet.
i think it's some curse.
i will always be the heartbroken,
never the heartbreaker.

so i will let you touch me
like all the boys have wanted to.
i will be everything you want
before my curse comes to us, to you.

i can't help wanting to try
before you leave me too.

♥

other girls

how many other girls
have kissed you,
how many others
have loved you before i have?

do i have no claim to you if they've loved you longer?
if they've kissed you more?
if they had you first?

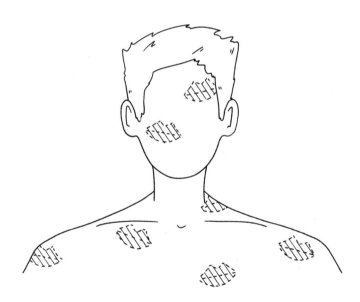

♥

burned the world when it landed

don't you know what happens to the boys
who love the poet?

don't you know how suffocating the pollen will be
when your bed is filled with flowers?
or how dirty the room will get
when love notes are covering the floor?

i will ruin you because
don't you know you're never going to love me more?

placeholder

what if i'm just a placeholder to you?
something to hold while you wait for time to pass.

i wonder if i'm like her at all,
the girl you couldn't have.

♥

love will come to me, again

love will come to me.
love will come to me.

i'm repeating it again.
i catch myself and stop.
i laugh. i laugh because
you're here. aren't you?

because sure,
love will come to me,
but love will not stay.

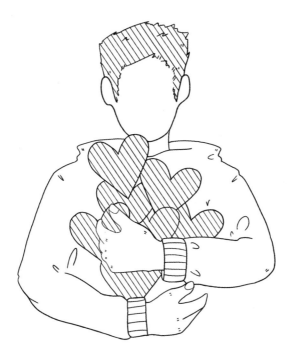

i already do

the prince of hearts
collects them.
he comes to me first.
he comes to the lover girl
and says,
would you love me, please,
and she replies with a sigh,
i already do.

your first love

i am not your first love.
i am not the first lips you kissed
nor the first hands you held in the hallway.
i am not the first to sit in the passenger side of your car.
i am not the first to hear your favorite song and
sing it with you under the stars.

when you tell me you love me now,
is she under every word?
when you tell me you love me,
do you remember how you loved her first?

bricks

i built bricks into my rib cage.
i filled it with cement
down to my chest, my lungs, my middle,
every open spot i had left.

no wolf will be able to blow it down.
not my heart.
not again.

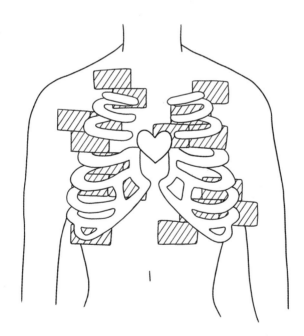

enjoying you

everything.
the way your skin feels
warm under the covers.
your legs against my own.
my cold feet on your hot skin.
it's perfect.
at least, it is for me.

but i'm just afraid
my perfect isn't yours
and that i'm enjoying you and
you're not enjoying me.

you shift away.

♥

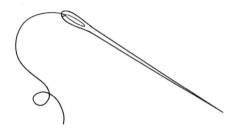

i want you to fix me

draw stitches between the places of my heart
that have not yet healed.
cover your hands with my blood,
my love,
and tell yourself
i'll be worth it when i'm done.
when you've fixed me.

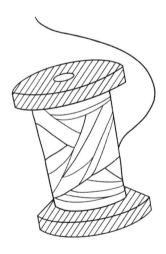

❤

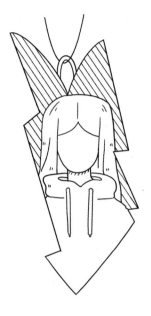

her

you messaged her today.
i saw her name on your phone.
her, her, her.

i never thought i'd be the kind of girlfriend
who's anxious over the *girl best friend*,
but here i am, i guess.
her.
it repeats inside my head like an echo,

and i can't say anything.
i can't tell you not to text her
or not to be friends with her.

♥

i can't say a word because
then i'd be just like every other
insecure girlfriend.
the girl who can't stand the thought
of her caring boyfriend
wanting anyone other than her.

but it's not her. it never really was.
it's just that i can't give you my trust,
my full heart,
because what if you break it?

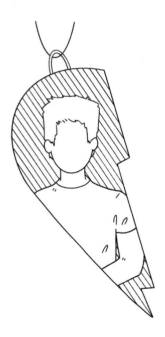
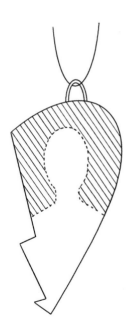

at any moment

when will you realize
that, even though you have me,
you can look at other girls if you want to?
nobody's stopping you.
i couldn't hold you down,
sew shut your eyes.
i couldn't stop you
even if i tried.

all you'd have to do is leave
if you wanted another love.

when will you realize
i'm easy to get rid of?

just enough

i can't text you.
i want to, but i won't.

it's what they told me. i'm too much.
i love too much, even to my friends.
they said it like this:
you take up all my time.

so i won't text you. that's too much.
i'll be better than i was.
i'll be your *just enough.*

♥

four

you've dated three girls before me,
and three doesn't seem bad,
it doesn't mean anything, really.

i just don't want to be "four."

parasite

i want to crawl through your mouth to your brain,
make a space there. just for me.

you cannot leave me
if i am so deeply burrowed into your life,
it would upset it to let me go.

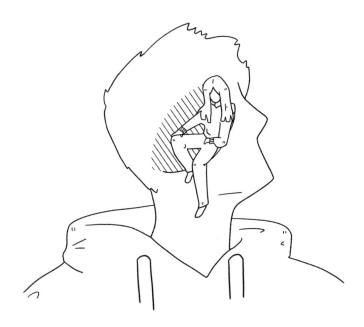

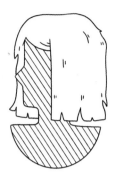

if i cut my hair

you wouldn't like me anymore if i cut my hair.

it seems silly, but i'd look different,
and you like me how i am.
i can't be different. it would change things, and
you said you like me how i am.
i don't want that to change.

you wouldn't like me anymore if i wore different
clothes, or different shoes.
you wouldn't like me if i didn't like
the tv shows you do
or if i showed you quirks
i hadn't revealed to you before.

♥

if i had the chance to start over with you,
i would lose you. i wouldn't be able to do it
because i'm already everything you don't like,
you just don't know it yet.

you wouldn't like me anymore if i cut my hair,
if you saw me any differently.

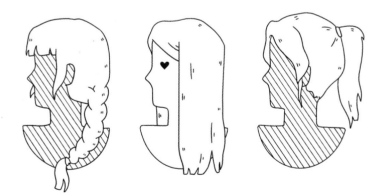

what you're thinking now

i'm so happy, and it's the same, because
i was so happy with him too.
when i was grinning,
what was on his mind?
how much time did he spend
planning out his goodbye?

you smile at me,
and i wonder if it'll always be the face of the guilty.

never into her

how long will it take
for me to start becoming
ugly to you?

how long will it take for you to say
you were never into me
just like you were never into her?

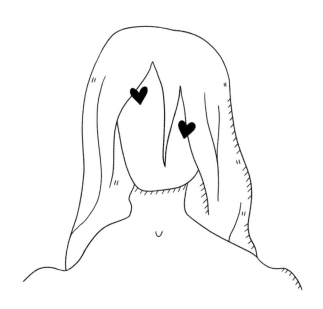

your friends

my best friend and her boyfriend
broke up today.
i saw it coming.
she'd been ready to leave him for
almost a month. she was just afraid.

and i support her, always, i'm happy for her,
but sometimes i wonder if you talk about me
to your friends like
she talked about him.
i wonder if your friends
hear all about how you want to leave me.

i wonder if they're rooting for you,
waiting for it to come.

and i wonder, if i were them,
if i heard how good my absence would be,

would i root for you too?

prettiest girl in the world

i will never be her,
your ex-girlfriend.
i will never be as pretty as her,
and even if you said i was,
you must see it in my eyes.
i don't believe you.

and you say it clearly, but
i'm made of daisies
that i've sewn into my hair and skin, and
they're rotting me.

you'll start to smell it soon.

i kiss them

when you kiss me,
i taste the vanilla lip balm of
every girl you've kissed before.
i feel them in the way you do it,
the way they taught you.

i kiss them while i
kiss you.

♥

ruin me for anyone else

break my heart.
ruin me. i won't mind, i promise.
i want it. i want you to take
every perfect piece of me and crumble it.
please, make me never want to fall in love again.

a broken heart will cure me.
doctors say it's medicine.

♥

you read my poetry

my friends don't read my poetry. nobody does, really.
not since i ripped myself in two
just for them
and they hated it.

you read my poetry.
you're the first to know since they did.

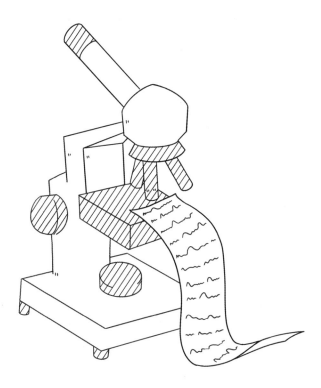

♥

a memory

your ex-girlfriend showed up on your
phone memories.
and my heart shouldn't be aching over
the girl you dated a year ago,
but here i am,
staring at the picture,
and you look so happy.

your hair is shorter. it's strange,
but your smile is still the same.
it's the same as when you look at me,
it's the same as when you tell me you love me.

❤

and now i'm wondering if you told her
you loved her like that too.

and i know it ended,
and i know it's just one photo
and you now have hundreds of me,
but i can't help it: staring,
wondering if one day
i'll be just a memory to you too.

♥

all i have is you

you have so many friends
and i—
if you left me, i'd be alone.

all i have is you, can't you see it?
you're all i have, and i think you know it,
and i think you hate it too.

sometimes, i worry that
the only reason you stay
is because you know that if you didn't,
it'd be the end of me.
because you know i'd be little miss lonely
without you by my side.

i wonder if you want to go.
i wonder if your guilt would let you say goodbye.

♥

leave me

i feel like a fool
because all i used to want was for him to
stay stay stay
and now i'm asking you to leave me
in the same way.
find someone new. set the fire.
burn me. i don't care.

because there's a certain comfort in
you leaving me too.
if it happened again,
at least i'd know what to do.

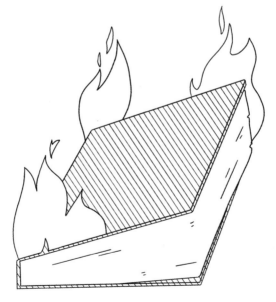

♥

your ex-girlfriend

i talked to her today.
she doesn't look like me at all,
not really,
but she's still the one who left you, isn't she?

i wonder if you were as heartbroken as me.
i wonder if you wrote poetry at stop signs
and cried in the car
on your way home.

sky in two

i've learned to not get too attached.
we'll break up eventually,
whether it be for college
or just because you stop liking me.
i ripped the sky in two and found you,
but what will i do when you're gone and
i'm left with nothing but a broken, watery view?

how tough it is to be happy, i guess,
when i can't stop falling in love.

♥

already let you go

i knew we had an expiration date,
circled it on the calendar.
i can be stronger this time.
i'll let it happen gently.

because if you left me now,
i wouldn't cry,
i wouldn't even be surprised.

i've no more tears left in my
pretty eyes.

broken mirror

i stare at myself like
breaking my mirror would
change my reflection and
distort the cracks i know will
soon reach my heart and bones.

every morning without you

i am sticky in the mornings without your touch.
like a baby, like a bird,
i am aching and tired.

those mornings, i wake up and imagine
i'll never touch you again.
those mornings, i practice the break of my bones.
i bead sweat on the back of my neck.

when you're not with me,
i pretend you never were.

♥

used to love me

i don't remember loving him.
i know i did.
i have all the poems to prove it,
but i can't recall the feeling, the ache in my soul,
that i describe with my little words,
because i know it happened,
but now love means nobody but you.

and i wonder if one day
you'll forget how it felt to love me
just like i have with him.
i wonder if one day
my love won't even be a memory,
just some awareness of a life you used to live,
of a girl you used to know.

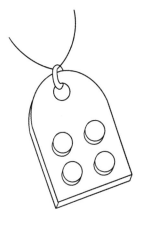

♥

my words

you haven't called me pretty in a week.
i don't know why it matters, why i'm counting,
but i dress up for you.
i want you to call me pretty, and if i look it, really,
you might.

and i know if i just asked you,
you'd say,
of course you are,
but i want you to say it without me asking.

i want you to say it like
they're not my words inside your mouth.

dependent

i can't live on my own.
my heart isn't strong enough anymore.

i can't live without someone to squeeze it for me,
pump my blood through my dying body,
breathe life into the pathetic fingers that
have forgotten how to write.

fight

i don't even want to think of the word.
i will not be in a relationship
that needs to be fixed.
we cannot *fight*,
i will not be broken. not again.

because i'm sick of
fighting and fixing
and it still not working.

and i know it's illogical for you
to never cry and
never frown with me nearby,
but i can't handle it.

please be perfect for me.

in your arms

i don't know if i've ever been as tired
as i've been between your arms.
i'm terrified, but
sometimes i wake up so comfortable,
you could move me with just your will,
because i can't stop the way i curl into you
like a secret i'm too afraid to tell.

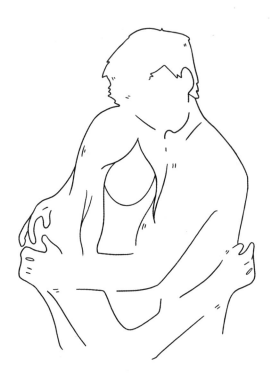

afraid to leave

i thought i was better,
i thought i was fixed.
you fixed me.

but here i am
in the bathroom, and
it's 12:28 in the morning, and
i'm too afraid to leave.

you disgust me, and i love you,
and i don't know what to do.

i can't kiss you. i can't kiss you.
i thought i was better, but
i can't kiss you.

raegan fordemwalt

fundamentally

what if, fundamentally,
we're not right for each other?
what if it's just pure luck that we're in love
and it's one of those cases
where you have to sleep with the radio on
and i can't stand it?
where there's a puzzle piece in our picture
that doesn't fit
and we just don't know yet
because we're not anywhere close
to finishing it.

♥

someone else

find someone else,
i'm begging you.
i can't handle it. handle this again.
and i know soon you'll realize it,
you'll look into my chest,
my heart,
and you'll hate what you find.

find someone else.
anyone else.
because right now you feel like you're mine.

to get you to go

i've been trying to get you to leave me.
small things.
i won't text you when i want to.
i won't reply for hours if i can.
i won't let it show.

i like you, but
you have to go,

because if i plan it out,
if i make it easy for you,
maybe it won't hurt. i won't be broken again.
maybe i won't have to know.

♥

all the pretty parts of her

lover girl can't seem to stop
loving people more than
they love her.

she's not built for relationships,
give and pull,
she just gives and gives
all the pretty parts of her
that cannot be returned.
that cannot be written in words.

but the prince of hearts
spreads it into him like he's dying.
as his blood blues, he
pumps it, drains it out,
and returns only a kiss to her lips
and a heart to her hand.

when we're alone

doesn't it mean
you don't love me
if you don't want me
like that
all of the time?

when we're alone,
it feels like you love me
even though you haven't touched me.

doesn't it mean
you don't love me
if you don't?

♥

i'm not them

you said,
i'm not them.
and i choked down
this terrifying realization

that you will not be like them.
my fingers shake.
you won't leave me too.

i'm panting. my eyes are watering
because you won't leave
and i believe it.

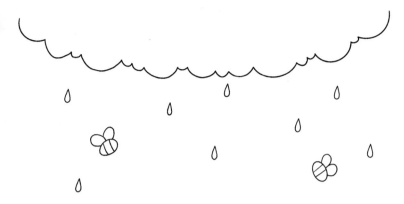

allowed to

i wrote you a poem about the rain.
i wrote about the bees,
and i wrote that i wasn't afraid.

and here i am,
soaked socks, swollen skin,
and wearing the shirt i almost forgot
to give back to you.

you were wrong.
i don't take up too much time.

i scream it because it's my story too.
i'm allowed to have loved you like i did.

i wrote about the rain.

not exciting anymore

it's not exciting anymore:
us.
we're not new. we're not the gossip,
we're not the flowers and first kisses
in the front seat of your car,
we're not dances and pretty dresses,
we're not short girl
and tall guy,
we're just us. you and i,
but i don't even mind.

god, i'll have you boring any day.
i'll have you just the way you are or
just the way it used to be,
it doesn't matter.
i'll have you all the same.

possible

you won't leave me.
that's *possible*.
there can be people that just don't want to leave.

you won't leave me.
and i believe it.

♥

confetti

confetti falls, and
i try to catch one before it reaches the ground.

my legs get lost in the rest of them.

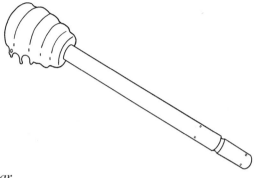

honey jar

i broke the honey jar.
i didn't mean to. if i wanted to break something,
i would have chosen something easier
to clean from the carpet,
but i didn't want to break something.
not tonight. i was with you,
but i made a mess. of course i did.

and it's going to take so much time,
the rest of your night.
isn't that what they said?
they told me
you take up all my time.

and so i've waited.
i've waited through each date you took me on,

♥

prince of hearts

each theater we went to,
each sunset we watched.
i've waited while you took me to dinner,
i've waited while you took me to prom
for you to tell me it too.
just like they did,
just like everyone had,
you'd say,
i've just grown tired of you.

and now i'm standing,
staring down at the honey jar,
ceramic,
honey bleeding on my elbow and
between my toes.
i'm stuck to the floor,
you're standing at the door, and i tell you

it's going to take
hours to get the honey off of me
and off of the floor,
glue the ceramic back together, and
pretend the issue is cured.

it's going to take
all your time,
the rest of the night,
to fix it.

♥

yes, you say.
you kiss the top of my head.
there's honey on your lips
and now dripping down into my eyes.

i don't mind.

5: everything is as it should be

prince of hearts

you're not the prince of hearts because
you stole mine.
that was easy—
well, at least it was for you.

no, you're the prince of hearts
because of what you did after.
you're my prince
because you gave me your heart too.

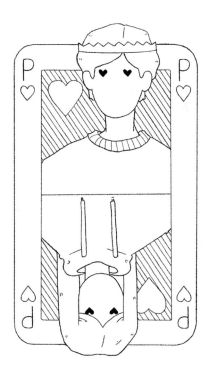

soulmates

i don't believe in soulmates.
i don't believe there's just one person
you're "destined" to be with.
i don't believe in disney
and how their princes and princesses are perfect
if they're together because
people aren't *meant* for each other.

call me a pessimist, but
it's not real.
love like that isn't real.

so of course
people aren't meant for each other,
but i do think
they become meant for each other
because
with all the time we've spent together,
everything we've been through,
we've learned how to complement each other's lives.

nobody's ever meant to be together,
but we're lucky we found each other,
someone who became the right
person for me
as i became the right person for you.

you were no prince, and i was no princess,
but i'm glad we wrote ourselves a love story,
even if it's just for us.

to the girl whose heart is broken

i never thought that after my ex-boyfriend
i could ever be happy again, and then
he came along.

and if he leaves,
i'll read this poem to remind myself
i can be.

you can be. breathe, hold it in.
you wrote this down. look at it.
look at it.

now read it again.

raegan fordemwalt

called it stars

i made a place for him.
i made everything.
i put a string around my heart and
watched as the balloon let confetti fall
while i called it shooting stars.
i watched as i loved more than me.
i wanted in agony,

and i would do it all again because,
if i just lifted my typing fingers,
i'd now be holding his hand.

just heartbreak

i will let myself love you
even if you hurt me
the exact same way.
even if you breathe their name.
even if you say,

you take up all my time.

even if you hate me by the end,
even if it's just another game,
i will let myself love you,
and i am not afraid.

it's just heartbreak. i can handle it.

gave me his

the prince of hearts
gave me his.
he said to hold on to it
for a while.
and he said it like he wanted me to.
he said it with a smile.

his heart will take only as much
as it needs.

my love is mine to give and keep.

someone

i know it seems like you need someone.
i know you're so sure that you need attention,
but you don't, and it's okay.
it's okay to not think about love
every minute of every day.
it doesn't make you any less of a lover.

not being in love does not mean
you never were
and never will be again.

listens

she rambles out her poetry like
vomit creeping up and out.
she spoils the floor, their bodies,
his mouth,
and the words she writes
cut into their throats
and break open their bones.

but the prince of hearts
holds the lover girl's hand
and listens.

all your time

would you mind if i took up
all your time?
i ask.

you smile, like it's the easiest thing in the world.
only as long as i get all your time too.

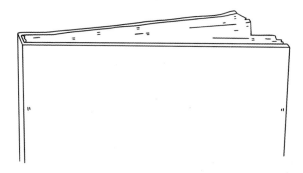

my poems

i showed you my poems,
and you said you liked them.
it felt like you really did because

you asked me to read them again.

♥

allowed to love

you're allowed to love him,
you know.
you're allowed to want that,
to want someone.

it's okay to love and want it back.

left me tomorrow

if you left me tomorrow
i'd want you back like it was consuming all of me.
i'd want you like you're the oxygen i breathe,
but
if you left me,
i'd hold my breath.
love is someone who wants me too.

if you left me,
i'd let you.

♥

visitor

maybe i'm a visitor in your heart.
many have come before me.
i can tell in the socks and the flowers
they've left behind here,
what a comfortable place, your heart. this room.

and i'd not mind visiting you forever,
making a home out of your
nearly wilting flowers and dirty laundry.
i dance on the coffee table.
i've already decorated the walls
with poetry and sticky notes.
it's all about you, everything i wrote,

because i'd visit you forever if you let me stick around.

lover

i like the idea that i am defined by
everything i ever loved.
i am my favorite books. i am my poetry.
i am the people who loved me back
and the people who didn't.
i am the love i gave that never got returned.

i am more than just loved.
i am a lover.

beside you

you don't know i'm writing this poem.
i'm beside you. i told you
i was *finishing a text*,
but i lied.
i hope you don't mind.

and you'll see this in a few days,
when i confess to you in the night
everything i now write.

i can't stop writing poetry about it
because it's the only way i can say
i love you
and have it sound right.

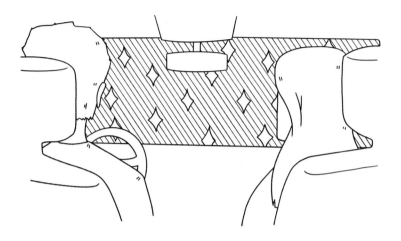

makeout point

and you took me to makeout point,
not to see the stars in the sky
but to see the city lights.

the world sparkled, and
now i'm here,
writing this poem
because you don't know
the only thing i was looking at was you.

can be loved

it's not that
because someone stopped loving you,
everyone will.
it's because someone
did love you
that you know you can be loved.
someone else can love you. you know that now.

♥

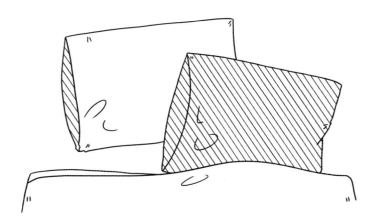

left side

i wasn't supposed to be here tonight.
i wasn't supposed to stay the night,
but you already had a pillow on the left side,
and you called it mine.

i sink into you like i don't know how not to.

any day now

you may just break my heart
any day now.
i can't control if you do.
i couldn't stop you, no matter how
perfectly i do my makeup or
how expensive my perfume.
you may just break my heart,
but i'll sign up for that risk every day
if it means i get you too.

who you are

who you're dating isn't
who you are.
i promise. his failures are not your own.

you are not him,
and that's okay.

your name

dear _____,
this poem is not for you.
i'm writing this because i think it's poetic.
i know you get it,
or at least the you i knew
said it like that too.

dear _____,
i don't want to tell you about my life,
or my love, or my anything.
those things aren't for you anymore.
and i'd rather not hear about yours, either.
your life after me.
your life during me.
i'd rather it stay a mystery. maybe then i can pretend it
didn't hurt when you left me,
that you were never a real friend
when we both know you probably were anyway.

dear _____. dear _____,
your name used to torture me.
it's everywhere.
i'd find it in the trees and the sidewalks.
i'd find it when i passed the street i used to turn onto
to drive to your house.
it doesn't bother me anymore.
i'm so proud because it doesn't bother me.

dear _____,
i'm only writing this poem
because it fits in the part of this story
where you never let me have a goodbye.

this is the goodbye,
and i hope you never read it.

♥

loving you isn't needing you

a part of me used to think
my codependency was a good thing.
if simplified, it just meant i really needed you,
really loved you
just like you loved me too.
it meant i'd put in my all again.
have you every moment.
never a lonely second,
but i've realized, this time,
i don't have to be around you.
i just want you.

i don't need you.
you're not oxygen in my lungs and blood.
i'm not bleeding between my thighs
or pretending you're made to be mine,
because i'm not screaming out your name.
i'm sighing it.

i breathe because
i can love you
and not need you.

weightless

he kissed me just as the elevator closed.
i felt my heart jump as my body moved up.
the weightlessness of the elevator dragged me down,
right to his arms.

down i went,
down into him.

♥

see you tonight

maybe there are other things i ought to be doing—
places i should be,
videos to make,
books to finish, but
i just wanted to see you tonight,
and you said you'd like to see me too.

♥

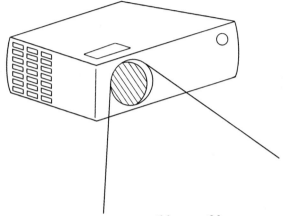

terrible, terrible you

i keep thinking about the things
i'll lose if you leave me.

like all my favorite songs i've shared with you
that you've endured listening to.
the feel of your hand in my own,
and playing *minecraft* on my phone.
i'd lose us reciting poetry late in the night
because the poems i can never get quite right
have always been about you.
terrible, terrible you.

♥

prince of hearts

i'll lose us
kissing in the back seat of my car
with the windows cracked,
for it's too hot in this summer air
to leave them closed.

i'll lose us
eating at that terrible breakfast place
we always do. where i spilled
apple juice all over myself on our first date,
and you took the photo that's still your lock screen.

i'll lose us
lying in your bed with that heavy blanket
you have. where the
smell of your sheets reminds me
of the taste of your lips
and the laughter from your family downstairs
is so nice.

and the pieces of my heart i tore out
just for you
that i'm just now making into art.
all these stupid poems i'm still writing,
trying to keep my head straight
about how much you mean to me.
how much i hate your eyes.
and all these wonderful things
i shall lose to you.
terrible, terrible you.

♥

and even if i lose you,
why would i want anyone else
to play *minecraft* with
or kiss
or spill apple juice on
or be terrible with
if i could do it with terrible, terrible you?

i give you my heart freely.
take it if you wish.

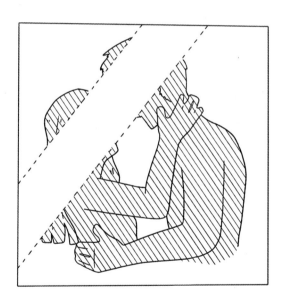

all her time

i traced your face with my fingernail.
the line of your cheek,
your brow bone,
each curve,
but this time,
when i closed my eyes,
you were not them.

like an old memory,
the love i had held on to still,
so strongly, so forcefully,
simply expelled out of my lungs.
it was gone,
they were gone,
and i am not the same as i was.

i breathe their names.

♥

raegan fordemwalt

my castle

you plucked the bricks i had placed
into my chest, one by one,

and i thought it would be you to save me,
but i tore the rest of it down on my own.

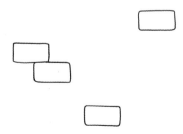

♥

love is terrible

love isn't supposed to be easy.
there's not going to be
a tube that can tie your heart to mine,
or a tree that lets our trunks intertwine.
love is so terrible, i reject it like a poison.
love makes my eyes hurt and my shoulders weak,
but every part of you that's terrible and
every fight we've had and
kiss when we've clinked teeth
are the most wonderful parts of it for me.

if you're loving easy, you're doing it wrong.

the prince and the poet

we look good together.
admit it, we do.
the prince and the poet,
with your smirk and my cheesy grin.
we look good together.
i know you know we do.

❤

special

i love you
so much,
but love isn't rare.
people fall in love all the time.
it's why we have a word for it, after all,
but i don't think you understand that i love you
so much.

and it's not like you haven't heard it before.
it's not like i'm the first one to ever
claim loving you,
to ever claim this stupid feeling,
it's more like

love not being rare doesn't make me feel
any less special being yours.

golden string

there is not a universe where
there is not a string tying you to me.

in every universe, somehow,
you'd find me.
somehow,
we'd find each other.

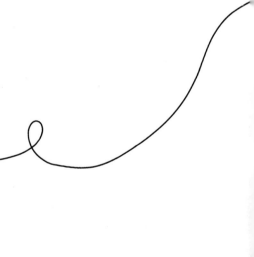

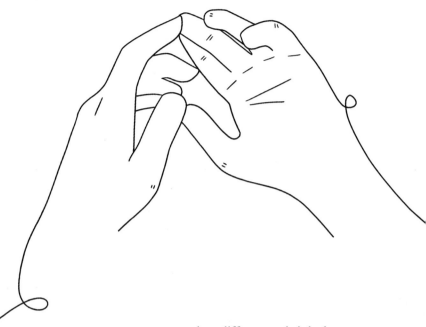

no matter how different my hair looks
or how my body is shaped,
we'd find each other

♥

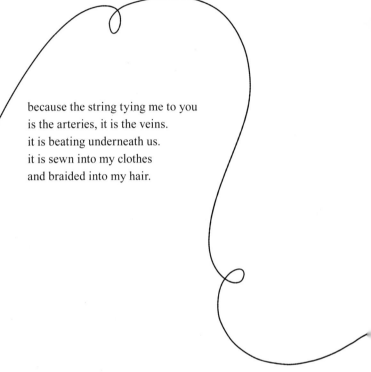

because the string tying me to you
is the arteries, it is the veins.
it is beating underneath us.
it is sewn into my clothes
and braided into my hair.

it is the roots of every tree.
it is buried in the earth, beating,
and it is inside you and me,
untangling until you meet me with a crash of our teeth
and the breath of your laughter as
my hair gets caught between your eyelashes.

in every lifetime,
every universe,
if we followed it back,
you'd find us, right here. you'd find me
reading this poem to you.

you'd find you, leaning down to kiss me in your car
before you take me home.
every time,
you say you love me,
and i say i know.

♥

i'd know to find you every time
because my soul ached in your absence before
it even knew you.

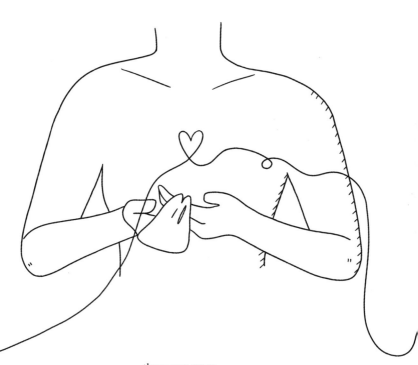

there you were,
and you found a place in my heart
that i didn't know needed to be filled.
there you were, and
it was as if you were somehow
always there.

and i tell you this late at night,
a mumble,
but i feel it in my chest that i'm right.
i look over to you, and
you're standing beside me like it's easy.

but i found you,
and you're here,

and everything is as it should be.

everything i've ever done
has led to you.
every heartbreak. every scar and star
has led to how you
kiss me now as confetti falls to the floor.

you're looking at me, and i know

everything is as it should be.

about the author

raegan fordemwalt is a poet from the vibrant city of boise, idaho, currently studying in california. she started writing poetry during her early teenage years and fell in love with the craft. she started posting her poetry online a few years later and found massive success on platforms like instagram and tiktok. throughout her year and a half of posting online, she gained more than four million followers and more than a hundred million likes and hearts across both platforms. raegan has inspired thousands of young writers to share their work online.

Prince of Hearts is her second published collection, a sequel to *Lover Girl*, released in 2024. she originally self-published *Lover Girl* as a senior in high school, and it reached #1 in multiple categories on amazon during its first week of publication. *Prince of Hearts* continues the story of heartbreak from its prequel, diving into the difficulties faced by a woman who is learning to trust again after going through a breakup.

raegan believes that poetry can be made from anything, whether that be a broken heart or just a weird pebble on the street. you can find more of her work online via her tiktok and instagram, @raeganspoetry.

♥